HEALTH AND FINANCE WEALTH FOR ELDERS

"Aging Gracefully, Investing Wisely: A Senior's Blueprint for Health and Financial Success"

BLESS P. WALTON

TABLE OF CONTENTS

CHAPTER 1

THE INTERSECTION OF HEALTH AND WEALTH

As seniors embark on the journey of aging gracefully and investing wisely, they are met with a profound realization—the intricate connection between health and wealth. In this chapter, we delve into the vital link between these two aspects of life, exploring the profound impact of lifestyle choices on long-term well-being and laying the foundation for holistic elderly health.

1.1 Understanding the Vital Link between Health and Finance

The symbiotic relationship between health and finance is a cornerstone of successful aging. Health and wealth are not isolated entities but rather dynamic elements that influence each other in profound ways. For seniors, recognizing this vital link is essential for crafting a retirement that is not only financially secure but also physically and mentally fulfilling.

Financial well-being contributes significantly to the quality of healthcare one can access. Adequate savings and insurance coverage empower seniors to address health challenges without the burden of financial stress. Conversely, maintaining good health is an investment that pays dividends in the form of reduced medical expenses and an enhanced ability to enjoy the fruits of one's labor in retirement.

Understanding the vital link between health and finance also involves recognizing the impact of healthcare costs on long-term financial plans. Medical expenses, including those related to prescription medications, doctor visits, and potential long-term care, can pose a significant threat to financial stability. Seniors must navigate these potential pitfalls with foresight and strategic financial planning.

As we explore this link, we'll examine case studies, expert insights, and real-world examples to illuminate the experiences of seniors who have successfully integrated health and wealth management into their retirement journey.

1.2 The Impact of Lifestyle Choices on Long-Term Well-being

The choices we make in our daily lives extend far beyond the present moment; they lay the groundwork for our long-term well-being. For seniors, lifestyle choices become even more pivotal as they navigate the challenges and opportunities of aging.

Diet, exercise, sleep, and stress management are key components of a healthy lifestyle that directly impact the aging process. In this section, we will delve into the science behind these choices, offering practical tips and evidence-based strategies for seniors to make informed decisions that promote not only longevity but also a high quality of life.

Moreover, we will explore the financial implications of lifestyle choices. Investing in preventive healthcare measures, such as regular health check-ups and wellness programs, can yield substantial long-term savings by mitigating the risk of more severe health issues that may require costly interventions.

Drawing on the expertise of nutritionists, fitness professionals, and healthcare specialists, this section aims to empower seniors to make lifestyle choices that align with their health and financial goals, fostering a holistic approach to well-being.

1.3 Setting the Foundation for Holistic Elderly Health

Holistic elderly health encompasses not only physical well-being but also mental and emotional wellness. As seniors transition into retirement, they face unique challenges that require a comprehensive approach to health—one that goes beyond medical check-ups and financial planning.

This section explores the importance of mental and emotional health in the context of aging. Topics such as social connections, purposeful living, and stress management will be discussed in detail, providing seniors with actionable strategies to cultivate resilience and joy in their golden years.

Additionally, we will address the role of preventive care in maintaining holistic health. Regular screenings, vaccinations, and lifestyle adjustments can significantly contribute to a senior's overall well-being, reducing the likelihood of health crises that may strain both physical and financial resources.

By setting the foundation for holistic elderly health, seniors can approach their retirement years with confidence, knowing that they have proactively addressed the interconnected aspects of health and wealth. Through expert advice, real-life stories, and practical tips, this section serves as a guide for seniors to create a robust foundation for a fulfilling and financially secure future.

CHAPTER 2

FINANCIAL WISDOM IN THE GOLDEN YEARS

As seniors embark on the path of aging gracefully and investing wisely, Chapter 2 illuminates the critical realm of financial wisdom in the golden years. Navigating retirement finances with confidence requires a nuanced understanding of budgeting, investment strategies, and maximizing income streams. In this chapter, we explore these essential elements, empowering seniors to cultivate financial resilience and security.

2.1 Navigating Retirement Finances with Confidence

Retirement marks a significant transition in one's financial journey, and navigating this terrain with confidence is paramount for a fulfilling and stress-free retirement. This section delves into the various facets of retirement finances, offering insights and strategies to empower seniors to make informed decisions.

Understanding the landscape of retirement accounts, such as 401(k)s, IRAs, and annuities, is crucial for optimizing financial resources. We will explore the benefits and considerations of each, providing a comprehensive guide to help seniors make choices aligned with their long-term goals.

Moreover, the chapter will address the importance of regular financial check-ups. Seniors will learn how to assess their financial health, identify potential areas for improvement, and adjust their strategies as needed. This proactive approach ensures that financial plans remain robust and adaptable to changing circumstances.

Case studies and real-life examples will be integrated to illustrate how seniors have successfully navigated the complexities of retirement finances. By drawing on the experiences of others, this section aims to demystify common challenges and instill confidence in seniors as they embark on this financial journey.

2.2 Crafting a Budget that Aligns with Senior Lifestyle Needs

Crafting a budget tailored to the unique needs and aspirations of seniors is a cornerstone of financial wisdom in the golden years. This section provides practical guidance on creating a budget that balances essential expenses, discretionary spending, and savings, ensuring financial stability throughout retirement.

We will explore the intricacies of budgeting for healthcare costs, travel expenses, and leisure activities, offering insights into cost-saving strategies without compromising on the quality of life. Additionally, the section will delve into the concept of an emergency fund tailored to the specific needs of seniors, providing a financial safety net for unexpected expenses.

Understanding the psychological and emotional aspects of budgeting is also crucial. Seniors will learn how to approach budgeting as a tool for empowerment rather than restriction, enabling them to align their financial resources with their values and priorities.

Through interactive exercises and budgeting templates, this section aims to make the budgeting process accessible and actionable. Seniors will gain the skills and confidence to proactively manage their finances, ensuring a sustainable and enjoyable lifestyle throughout their golden years.

2.3 Maximizing Social Security and Pension Benefits

Social Security and pension benefits represent valuable income streams for seniors, and maximizing these resources is a key component of financial wisdom in retirement. In this section, we explore strategies to optimize Social Security and pension benefits, providing seniors with the knowledge to make informed decisions.

Understanding the intricacies of Social Security, including when to claim benefits and the impact of delaying retirement, is essential for maximizing its potential. Seniors will learn how to navigate the system effectively, considering factors such as life expectancy and individual financial needs.

Pension benefits, if available, add another layer to the financial puzzle. This section delves into strategies for maximizing pension income, exploring options such as lump-sum payments, joint and survivor annuities, and other considerations that align with individual circumstances.

Throughout this exploration, real-life stories and expert insights will be integrated to illustrate successful approaches to maximizing Social Security and pension benefits. By drawing on the experiences of others, seniors can gain practical insights that enhance their own financial decision-making.

In conclusion, Chapter 2 serves as a comprehensive guide to financial wisdom in the golden years. Seniors will gain the knowledge and tools to navigate retirement finances with confidence, craft a budget that aligns with their lifestyle needs, and maximize their Social Security and pension benefits for a secure and fulfilling retirement.

CHAPTER 3

PHYSICAL WELLNESS STRATEGIES FOR SENIORS

In the pursuit of aging gracefully and investing wisely, Chapter 3 focuses on the indispensable aspect of physical wellness for seniors. As bodies undergo natural changes with age, proactive health measures, customized exercise regimens, and mindful nutrition become vital components of a holistic approach to aging. This chapter serves as a guide, offering seniors actionable strategies to enhance their physical well-being and embrace the golden years with vitality.

3.1 Proactive Health Measures for Aging Bodies

Proactive health measures lay the foundation for a resilient and thriving senior lifestyle. In this section, we explore the importance of preventive care and routine health screenings, emphasizing the role of early detection in managing potential health issues effectively.

Regular health check-ups, including screenings for common age-related conditions such as heart disease, diabetes, and osteoporosis, become crucial tools in maintaining optimal health. Through expert insights and real-life examples, seniors will gain an understanding of the significance of early intervention and its positive impact on long-term well-being.

Furthermore, we delve into the importance of vaccination for seniors. Immunizations against influenza, pneumonia, and other preventable diseases play a vital role in safeguarding senior health, reducing the risk of complications and hospitalization.

This section aims to empower seniors with the knowledge and resources needed to take charge of their health proactively. By adopting a preventive mindset, seniors can enhance their overall well-being and enjoy a higher quality of life in their golden years.

3.2 Exercise Regimens Tailored for Elderly Fitness

Tailoring exercise regimens to suit the specific needs and abilities of aging bodies is a cornerstone of physical wellness for seniors. This section explores the diverse benefits of regular physical activity, offering guidance on customized exercise programs that enhance strength, flexibility, and cardiovascular health.

We delve into low-impact exercises that are gentle on joints while still providing significant health benefits. Strength training, balance exercises, and flexibility routines become essential components of a well-rounded fitness plan, designed to address the specific challenges that seniors may face.

The chapter also explores the importance of staying active in daily life, incorporating movement into routine activities, and embracing enjoyable forms of exercise. From walking and swimming to yoga and tai chi, seniors will discover a range of options that cater to their individual preferences and physical conditions.

Real-life success stories of seniors who have embraced tailored exercise regimens serve as inspiration and motivation. Through these narratives, seniors can envision the positive impact of regular physical activity on their own lives, fostering a sense of empowerment and possibility.

3.3 Nutrition and Diet Tips for Longevity

A well-balanced and nutritious diet is a fundamental pillar of physical wellness for seniors. In this section, we explore the role of nutrition in promoting longevity, preventing chronic diseases, and supporting overall health and vitality.

Seniors will gain insights into age-appropriate dietary guidelines, including recommendations for essential nutrients such as calcium, vitamin D, and fiber. We also discuss the importance of hydration, as adequate water intake becomes increasingly crucial for various bodily functions in later years.

Moreover, the chapter addresses the challenges and opportunities related to dietary choices, including managing weight, addressing food sensitivities, and adapting to changing nutritional needs. Practical tips on meal planning, grocery shopping, and cooking strategies tailored for seniors are provided to make healthy eating a manageable and enjoyable part of daily life.

Real-world examples of seniors who have transformed their health through mindful nutrition underscore the transformative power of dietary choices. By incorporating these insights into their own lives, seniors can embark on a journey of nutritional well-being that complements their physical fitness goals and contributes to a vibrant and fulfilling retirement.

In conclusion, Chapter 3 serves as a comprehensive guide to physical wellness strategies for seniors. By embracing proactive health measures, tailored exercise regimens, and mindful nutrition, seniors can optimize their physical well-being, fostering a sense of vitality and resilience that enhances their overall quality of life in the golden years.

CHAPTER 4

BUILDING AND SAFEGUARDING WEALTH IN RETIREMENT

In the pursuit of aging gracefully and investing wisely, Chapter 4 delves into the crucial realm of building and safeguarding wealth in retirement. This chapter explores investment strategies for sustainable financial growth, the importance of diversification and risk management in senior portfolios, and the necessity of adapting financial plans to changing health needs.

By addressing these key aspects, seniors can navigate the complexities of financial planning with confidence, ensuring their wealth aligns with their evolving lifestyle and health requirements.

4.1 Investment Strategies for Sustainable Financial Growth

As seniors transition into retirement, the dynamics of investment strategies undergo a transformation. The focus shifts from wealth accumulation to sustainable financial growth that can support a comfortable and secure lifestyle throughout the golden years. In this section, we explore investment strategies tailored to the unique needs and goals of seniors.

We delve into the concept of a balanced portfolio that combines conservative and growth-oriented investments. This approach allows seniors to benefit from potential market gains while mitigating the impact of market volatility on their wealth. Asset allocation, including a mix of stocks, bonds, and alternative investments, becomes a key consideration for achieving sustainable financial growth.

Furthermore, the chapter explores income-generating investments such as dividends, bonds, and real estate. Seniors will gain insights into creating a steady income stream that aligns with their financial needs and aspirations. The importance of periodic portfolio reviews and adjustments to accommodate changing market conditions and personal goals is emphasized.

Real-life case studies and expert perspectives provide practical examples of successful investment strategies for seniors. By understanding the principles of sustainable financial growth, seniors can make informed decisions that contribute to a resilient and thriving retirement.

4.2 Diversification and Risk Management in Senior Portfolios

Diversification and risk management are paramount considerations for senior portfolios aiming to safeguard wealth and foster long-term financial success. This section explores the importance of spreading investments across various asset classes to minimize risk and optimize returns.

We delve into the concept of diversification, illustrating how a well-balanced portfolio can withstand market fluctuations more effectively than a concentrated one. Seniors will gain insights into building a diversified portfolio that aligns with their risk tolerance, time horizon, and financial goals.

Risk management strategies, including the use of protective measures such as stop-loss orders and insurance products, are examined to provide seniors with tools for mitigating potential financial setbacks. Understanding the interplay between risk and return becomes crucial for making investment decisions that align with individual circumstances.

The chapter also addresses the role of professional financial advice in diversification and risk management. Seniors will gain an understanding of how working with financial advisors can provide personalized insights and strategies to navigate the complexities of the financial landscape.

Real-world examples highlight the impact of effective diversification and risk management on senior portfolios. By learning from the experiences of others, seniors can implement these principles into their own financial plans, fostering a sense of security and confidence in the face of market uncertainties.

4.3 Adapting Financial Plans to Changing Health Needs

One of the unique challenges seniors face in retirement is the potential impact of changing health needs on their financial plans. This section explores the necessity of adapting financial strategies to accommodate evolving health circumstances, ensuring that wealth remains a supportive resource rather than a source of stress.

We delve into the role of health savings accounts (HSAs) and long-term care insurance as components of a comprehensive financial plan. Seniors will gain insights into how these tools can help address healthcare costs and provide a safety net for unexpected medical expenses.

Moreover, the chapter explores the concept of dynamic financial planning that considers the intersection of health and wealth. Seniors will learn how to adjust their financial plans in response to changes in health, from medical treatments to potential modifications in lifestyle and living arrangements.

Real-life stories of seniors who have successfully adapted their financial plans to changing health needs serve as inspiration and guidance. By understanding the importance of flexibility and foresight, seniors can proactively navigate the intersection of health and wealth, ensuring that their financial plans remain resilient and responsive to the challenges of aging.

In conclusion, Chapter 4 serves as a comprehensive guide to building and safeguarding wealth in retirement. By implementing sustainable investment strategies, embracing diversification and risk management, and adapting financial plans to changing health needs, seniors can navigate the complexities of financial planning with confidence and resilience, ensuring their wealth supports a fulfilling and secure retirement.

CHAPTER 5

ACHIEVING A HARMONIOUS RETIREMENT LIFESTYLE

As seniors embark on the journey of aging gracefully and investing wisely, Chapter 5 explores the crucial aspect of achieving a harmonious retirement lifestyle. This chapter delves into the delicate balance of leisure, hobbies, and social connections, smart and enriching travel experiences, and the cultivation of a resilient mindset for a fulfilling retirement. By addressing these elements, seniors can navigate their golden years with purpose, joy, and a sense of fulfillment.

5.1 Balancing Leisure, Hobbies, and Social Connections

Retirement offers the gift of time, and how seniors choose to spend this time significantly influences their overall well-being. In this section, we delve into the art of balancing leisure, engaging in meaningful hobbies, and fostering social connections to create a fulfilling and harmonious retirement lifestyle.

Leisure activities play a pivotal role in promoting relaxation and joy. Seniors will explore the importance of incorporating activities they are passionate about into their daily lives, whether it's reading, gardening, painting, or enjoying the arts. We also discuss the value of trying new activities to discover untapped interests and talents.

Hobbies become an avenue for personal expression and self-discovery. The chapter provides guidance on selecting hobbies that align with individual interests and abilities, ensuring that they contribute positively to mental and emotional well-being. Real-life stories of seniors who have found purpose and joy through their hobbies serve as inspiration for readers.

Social connections are essential components of a harmonious retirement lifestyle. Seniors will gain insights into the importance of maintaining existing relationships and fostering new connections. We explore various avenues for social engagement, from community groups and volunteering to digital platforms that connect like-minded individuals.

The concept of a balanced social calendar is discussed, highlighting the need for a mix of solitary and social activities. By striking the right balance, seniors can cultivate a rich and fulfilling social life that contributes to their overall sense of well-being.

5.2 Traveling Smartly: Exploring the World in Your Golden Years

Travel is a powerful way for seniors to broaden their horizons, create lasting memories, and embrace new experiences. This section explores the art of traveling smartly, providing practical insights on planning enriching and stress-free journeys that align with the unique needs of seniors.

We delve into considerations such as health and safety while traveling, adapting to different climates and time zones, and managing travel-related expenses. Seniors will gain insights into creating travel itineraries that balance adventure and relaxation, ensuring a well-rounded and enjoyable experience.

The chapter also explores travel options that cater to various preferences and mobility levels, from cultural city explorations to scenic cruises and relaxing beach getaways. Real-life stories of seniors who have embraced travel as a central component of their retirement lifestyle provide inspiration and guidance for those looking to embark on similar journeys.

Additionally, the section addresses the concept of purposeful travel, incorporating elements of cultural immersion, volunteerism, and lifelong learning. By approaching travel with intention, seniors can derive deeper meaning and satisfaction from their experiences.

5.3 Cultivating a Resilient Mindset for a Fulfilling Retirement

The mindset with which seniors approach their retirement years significantly influences their overall satisfaction and well-being. In this section, we explore the concept of cultivating a resilient mindset, offering insights and strategies to navigate the inevitable challenges and changes that come with aging.

We delve into the importance of embracing adaptability and a positive outlook. Seniors will gain tools for reframing challenges as opportunities for growth, fostering a mindset that promotes resilience and a sense of empowerment. Real-life examples of seniors who have navigated life's transitions with grace and resilience serve as inspiration.

The chapter also explores the role of mindfulness and gratitude in cultivating a resilient mindset. Seniors will learn practical techniques for staying present, managing stress, and fostering a sense of appreciation for the moments that matter. The concept of lifelong learning and staying intellectually engaged is also discussed, contributing to a mindset of continuous growth and curiosity.

Additionally, we address the importance of seeking support when needed, whether through social connections, professional counseling, or community resources. By building a strong support network, seniors can face challenges with resilience and maintain a sense of well-being throughout their retirement journey.

In conclusion, Chapter 5 serves as a comprehensive guide to achieving a harmonious retirement lifestyle. By balancing leisure, engaging in enriching hobbies, fostering social connections, traveling smartly, and cultivating a resilient mindset, seniors can navigate their golden years with purpose and fulfillment.

This chapter aims to empower seniors to embrace the opportunities and challenges of retirement, fostering a sense of joy and contentment in this transformative phase of life.